Rodrigo Mazer Etto
Valeska G. Carlos

Happy old year: the crisis in the Brazilian prison system in 2017

Rodrigo Mazer Etto
Valeska G. Carlos

Happy old year: the crisis in the Brazilian prison system in 2017

ScienciaScripts

Imprint
Any brand names and product names mentioned in this book are subject to trademark, brand or patent protection and are trademarks or registered trademarks of their respective holders. The use of brand names, product names, common names, trade names, product descriptions etc. even without a particular marking in this work is in no way to be construed to mean that such names may be regarded as unrestricted in respect of trademark and brand protection legislation and could thus be used by anyone.

Cover image: www.ingimage.com

This book is a translation from the original published under ISBN 978-3-330-20002-9.

Publisher:
Sciencia Scripts
is a trademark of
Dodo Books Indian Ocean Ltd. and OmniScriptum S.R.L publishing group

120 High Road, East Finchley, London, N2 9ED, United Kingdom
Str. Armeneasca 28/1, office 1, Chisinau MD-2012, Republic of Moldova, Europe
Printed at: see last page
ISBN: 978-620-8-26675-2

Summary

Happy Old Year: the crisis of the Brazilian Penitentiary System in 2017.

Summary

This book discusses some of the factors that contribute to the chaos in the Brazilian prison system, which once again attracted worldwide attention with numerous riots at the beginning of 2017. Using the research methodology of documentary analysis and bibliographic review, this volume aims to address some of the issues that contribute to the prison problem in Brazil, such as the issue of human rights and the legal guarantees of prisoners - involving prison overcrowding and the precarious conditions of prison units; the recurring problem of lack of security due to the constant prisoner rebellions and escapes - especially those that occurred in the first fifteen days of this year; the health care and treatment of inmates, according to various studies carried out in the prison context - such as Pinese (2008), who studied the high incidence of cases of depression among the prison population, Santos (2002) and Bezerra (2015), who found a large number of inmates with HIV, and Sanchez (2007) and Lima (2015), who identified a high percentage of inmates infected with tuberculosis. The phenomenon of criminal and prison recidivism will also be discussed, using data from the most recent IPEA survey as a parameter (BRASIL, 2015b). Finally, through the latest survey of the National Socio-Educational Care System (BRASIL, 2015c) and the 2016 data from the National Register of Adolescents in Conflict (CNJ, 2016), the delicate situation of the large number of adolescents serving socio-educational measures of deprivation of liberty in Brazil was addressed. In order to provide a critical reflection on the reality of Brazilian prisons, this book uses various documents that deal with the criminal execution process, such as the Brazilian Constitution of 1988 (BRASIL, 1988), the Criminal Execution Law, the Law on Heinous Crimes (BRASIL, 1990a), the Anti-Drug Law (BRASIL, 2006), and some data obtained by international organizations such as the American Declaration of the Rights and Duties of Man (BOGOTA, 1948) and the Report of the Subcommittee on the Prevention of Torture (UN, 2016).

INTRODUCTION

2017 began with a new chapter in an old story: the chaos of the Brazilian prison system. The first fifteen days of the year were marked by violent riots in thirteen of the country's Prison Units, which left a total of 138 inmates dead and raised countless discussions both in terms of security policies and social policies, drawing attention to the fragility of the national prison system.

In just over two weeks, there have been violent uprisings by prisoners in units all over the country: the state of Amazonas suffered riots in two prisons and in a public jail; Roraima faced a violent massacre in a prison unit; the state of Rio Grande do Norte also faced a rioted unit and prison units in the states of Paraiba, Alagoas, Parana and Sao Paulo were also surprised by violent riots, which left many dead and injured.

According to the most recent survey of prison information - INFOPEN (2014), from 2000 to December 2014, the Brazilian prison population increased by 167%, and in the last 20 years, the number of Brazilian prisoners has increased by more than 400%, leading Brazil to occupy the fourth position in the ranking of countries with the largest prison population, behind the United States, China and Russia, respectively. "If this trend continues, it can be projected that the population deprived of liberty in Brazil will surpass that of Russia in 2018" (INFOPEN, 2014, p. 14-15).

For the sake of comparison, in order to make it easier to understand Brazil's delicate prison situation, in 2014 India had 1,236,344,631 inhabitants and a prison population of 418,536 prisoners; in contrast, for a total population of 202.768,562 inhabitants (IBGE, 2014), the Brazilian prison population was 622,202 (INFOPEN, 2014), i.e. Brazil, despite having six times fewer inhabitants than India, had almost 200,000 more prisoners.

Considering the large number of prisoners in Brazil and with the aim of reflecting on some critical points in the national prison system, which culminated in the tragic events of early 2017, this book, using documentary research methodology, is divided into five parts.

The first deals with the issue of the human rights of prisoners, in which a discussion will be held on the concept of human rights and their real application to the prison context, according to the definitions contained in the Penal Execution Law (BRASIL, 1984), the Law of Heinous Crimes (BRASIL, 1990b), the Law of Introduction to the Norms of Law (BRASIL, 2010), the Brazilian Federal Constitution (BRASIL, 1988), the 1st United Nations Congress on the Prevention of Crime and the Treatment of Offenders (UN, 1955), the American Declaration of the Rights and Duties of Man (BOGOTA, 1948), the Report of the Subcommittee on the Prevention of Torture and Other Cruel, Inhuman and Degrading Treatment or Punishment (UN, 2016), and especially the Universal Declaration of Human Rights (UN, 1948). This first section will also deal with the problem of the dehumanization of sentences, through the theoretical framework of Foucault (1999), in which the positions of Erving Goffman (1974) will be listed in relation to the concept of total institution.

The second section of this book deals with the social problems of the mass escapes and 13 rebellions that made national and world press headlines in the first half of 2017, which resulted in 131 inmates being murdered. The main reasons for these violent and sudden uprisings will be presented, such as the overcrowding of cells, the lack of separation between high-risk prisoners and ordinary prisoners, the precarious security conditions in prisons and the poor structural conditions of prison units.

The third part of this volume will raise some issues related to the health care of prisoners, considering the provisions contained in the laws that regulate this situation, such as the Penal Execution Law (BRASIL, 1984) and the Universal Declaration of Human Rights (UN, 1948); and the data from research that addresses the main diseases that affect prisoners in the prison environment, such as AIDS (SANTOS, 2002) and (BEZERRA, 2015), tuberculosis (SANCHEZ, 2007), (BORGES, 2014) and (LIMA, 2015), hepatitis (GUIMARAES, 1998), depression (PINESE, 2008) and mental disorders (FONTE, 2011) and (MARQUES, 2013).

The fourth part of the book presents the results of a survey on the phenomenon of criminal and prison recidivism in Brazil, taking into account the high rate of recidivism demonstrated by the data collected in a recent survey carried out by the Institute of Applied Economic Research (BRASIL, 2015b). In conclusion, the Patronato Penitenciario and its legally established functions will be presented, as well as the problem of the ineffectiveness of the resocializing model of the national penitentiary system.

Based on official documents, the fifth point to be covered in this book presents some definitions of the concept of adolescence, according to the Statute of Children and Adolescents (BRASIL, 1990b), the World Health Organization (WHO, 1986) and the Pan American Health Organization (PAHO, 2012), showing the high percentage of adolescents serving socio-educational measures of deprivation of liberty, due to the practice of infractions, considering that many adolescent offenders end up persisting in criminal practices, ending their life trajectories in penitentiaries, when they reach adulthood.

I. Human rights and legal guarantees for prisoners

Discussions about the chaos in the Brazilian prison system go beyond the issue of security and violence in the units, calling into question the political and social role that the prison system should play. Crime and punishment have always played a political role in society, which has often accepted violent punitive practices, such as torture, represented by cruel scourging of the human body. However, the substitution of the death penalty for the custodial sentence in modern society has not changed its marginalizing and punitive character; on the contrary, it has, in a sense, characterized a pseudo-humanization of punishment. That said, Ana Maria de Barros states

> Society, frightened by the rise in violence, expects prison to be a place of punishment and atonement for the criminal. The maintenance of this feeling of atonement, common in ancient and current societies, is aggravated by the growth in violent crime, especially when crime statistics point to victims in the more affluent sections of the population (2011, p. 04).

Reading the book *"Surveillance and Punishment: Birth of the Prison",* written by the French philosopher Paul-Michel Foucault, it is possible to understand that it was from the end of the 18th century that a phase of humanization of punishment began. This stage was inaugurated when the right to punish shifted from the revenge of the sovereign to the defense of society, based on the idea that "punishment must have humanity as its measure" (FOUCAULT, 1999, p.70).

In this new process of humanization, the violent punitive practices applied to the body of the lawbreaker have become unviable and unacceptable to the values of a modern society, because nowadays, there is a value attached to the individual, according to the prevailing economic logic: there is a valuation of the body, and it is necessary for the individual/body to be trained and disciplined, according to norms established by various social institutions such as, for example, the school, the family, among others. With regard to this change in the concept of humanization, through the discipline of the individual's body, Foucault explains that it is due to

> [...] a discovery of the body as an object and target of power. We can easily find signs of the great attention then paid to the body - to the body that is manipulated, shaped, trembled, that obeys, responds, becomes skilled or whose forces multiply.

(FOUCAULT, 1999, p.117).

Within this new way of looking at the individual, punitive methods that only affected the body, causing suffering through physical pain, were deemed unviable. In this way, a reorganization of punitive practices emerged in which it was not the body of the individual who was punished that was marked, but rather their soul, showing that the new power to punish was no longer visible on the subject's body, but encompassed their subjectivity (FOUCAULT, 1999).

Although the debate on the humanization of sentencing conditions began a long time ago, there are still many issues that require a deeper reflection on the conditions and purposes of the Brazilian Penitentiary System.

In this sense, the Canadian sociologist Erving Goffman developed the work *"Asylums, Prisons and Convents"*, whose notes help to think about the institutionalized 'dehumanization' in prisons. The author focuses his observations on the subjectivity of the inmate, interested in analyzing how the condition of being imprisoned (re)structures the subject in deprivation of liberty (GOFFMAN, 1974). Instead of the term 'prison', this sociologist prefers to use the expression 'total institution', as being

> [...] a place of residence and work where a large number of similarly situated individuals, separated from the wider society for a considerable period of time, lead a closed and formally administered life (GOFFMAN, 1974, p.11).

Total institutions are characterized by the separation of individuals from society, through their total submission to an institutional administration. Such conditions of social segregation cause various transformations in the inmates, both in their personal context and in their social role, and these changes are called by Goffman *'mortification'* - a process in which the personal element of the subject, the singular, his *"self"* is desecrated and deconstructed by the influence of the institution's standardization, since, on entering a *"total institution"*, the individual in prison is automatically subordinated to the institution's objectives, and there is no room for the manifestation of his personal identity (GOFFMAN, 1974).

As this book seeks to present a reflection on the precarious and inhumane conditions of the prison units belonging to the National Penitentiary System with the consequent problem of the wave of rebellions, it becomes essential to review the literature that addresses the relationship between the prison system and human rights, considering that the understanding of the expression *'Penitentiary System'* comes from Law No. 7.210, of July 11, 1984, the Penal Execution Law (BRASIL, 1984).

Thus, this volume conceives the Penitentiary System as a set of administrative measures and institutions, such as: police stations, where the subject awaits his trial; medical-penal complexes, where subjects who need psychiatric and outpatient treatment are detained; and penitentiaries, where subjects who have already been tried are held, which are called by numerous synonyms such as detention center, prison, house of custody, among others (DEPEN, 2014).

Thus, the Penitentiary System is characterized as the executor of custodial sentences with the aim of re-socializing the institutionalized subject, and the architectural standards of its prisons are also governed by legal norms, such as the Penal Execution Law (BRASIL, 1984).

Despite being widely disseminated in the media, the term *'human rights'* is fluid, wide open and under constant construction, and its definition is complex.

According to Orth (2012), human rights are historically and socially instituted, resulting from political agreements that legitimize them. Therefore, it is a mistake to consider human rights as a product of human nature, because, despite their normative nature, these rights are susceptible to changes related to social transformations, and reflect the desires and customs of a given society.

This position coincides with the opinion of Ventura (2010), for whom human rights are a universal parameter, originating in international law and encompassing the fields of legal rights and ethics. Human rights thus qualify and reinforce the moral demand for respect and dignity for human beings.

Another similar position is that defended by Mello (2001, p. 33), who defines human rights as *"the set of norms that establish the rights that human beings possess for the development of their personality and establish mechanisms for the protection of such rights[1] ".*

The long and violent history of the struggle for citizenship shows that only civil and political rights were recognized as rights of the individual, but gradually, since 1950, with the progress of democracy, the definition of human rights has also included cultural, social and economic rights.

Currently, the main document for the implementation and dissemination of human rights in the world is the *"Universal Declaration of Human Rights*[1] " (UN, 1948), and it was through this document that health, whether physical, psychological or emotional, was conceived as a right, although many countries apply these recommendations according to their convenience and reality.

In this way, the rights described in this UN document are interpreted and implemented in different ways, according to the political and social determinations of the different world governments, which clearly demonstrates that this concept is under permanent construction.

With the end of the obscure dictatorial period[2] in Brazil, the Brazilian state began to pay more attention to guaranteeing citizens' rights, and it was precisely at this time that the term *"citizenship"* began to be widely used by the press and civil society, in other words, *"citizenship literally fell into the mouths of the people. What's more, it replaced the people themselves in political rhetoric. We no longer say 'the people want this or that', we say 'the citizenry wants it'. Citizenship has become people""* (CARVALHO, 2002, p. 07).

Although Brazilians had high expectations that they would have all their rights guaranteed with the advent of the 1988 Federal Constitution, after its implementation

The only rights that were really in force were those related to political organization, expression, freedom and participation, and the other rights, such as social and labor rights, were not fully established. As a result, different categories of citizens emerged: those who had full or partial access to rights, and those who were excluded from

[2] The period of military dictatorship in Brazil began on March31, 1964, with the military coup that overthrew then president Joao Goulart and ended on January 15, 1985, with the election of Tancredo Neves to the presidency of Brazil. This period was characterized by countless violations of the rights of Brazilian citizens, such as the revocation of political rights of opponents of the regime, repression of social movements and demonstrations of opposition to the government, censorship of the media and the use of torture methods against opponents of the military regime.

access to their rights, as Carvalho (2002) points out.

> It has become customary to divide citizenship into civil, political and social rights. A full citizen would be one who had all three rights. Incomplete citizens would be those who possessed only some of the rights. Those who did not benefit from any of the rights would be non-citizens. [...] If civil rights guarantee life in society, if political rights guarantee participation in the government of society, social rights guarantee participation in collective wealth. They include the right to education, to work, to a fair wage, to health and to retirement. The guarantee of their validity depends on the existence of an efficient administrative machinery in the executive branch. In theory, they can exist without civil rights and certainly without political rights. They can even be used as a substitute for political rights. But in the absence of civil and political rights, their content and scope tend to be arbitrary. Social rights allow politically organized societies to reduce the excesses of inequality produced by capitalism and guarantee a minimum level of well-being for all. The central idea on which they are based is that of social justice (CARVALHO, 2002, p. 9-10).

Within this social division, which distinguishes between citizens who fully enjoy their rights, and individuals who do not have access to the same rights, the problem of individuals imprisoned due to judicial convictions arises. How can we think about the citizenship of incarcerated individuals? The answer to this question is complex, because contrary to what is expected, the current conditions of the Brazilian Penitentiary System stimulate and produce an increase in violence, contributing to the process of social stigmatization of the incarcerated and conditioning them to deep and inhuman suffering.

The human rights and guarantees of people deprived of their liberty are legally provided for in statutes and documents, both at federal and international level.

At the national level, in addition to the Penal Execution Law (BRASIL, 1984) and the Law of Introduction to the Norms of Law (BRASIL, 2010), the Magna Carta (BRASIL, 1988), in its Article 5, has 32 sections that deal with the protection of the fundamental guarantees of the imprisoned man.

Articles XI, XII, XVIII and XXVI of Chapter One of the American Declaration of the Rights and Duties of Man (BOGOTA, 1948) and the UN Resolutions (1955, 2016) are examples of international conventions that lay down minimum rules for the treatment of incarcerated people.

The set of Brazilian regulations dealing with the rights and duties of prisoners (BRASIL, 1984; 1988; 2010) is considered to be one of the most advanced and democratic ever created. It is based on the concept that the execution of custodial sentences must be based on the principle of humanity, and any type of unnecessary, degrading or cruel punishment will be considered inhumane and contrary to the principle of legality.

However, the media has reported on the constant violation of the rights of prisoners and the total lack of respect for the legal guarantees provided for in the execution of custodial sentences.

In this sense, it is important to point out that, when they come under the protection of the state, the individual sentenced to a closed sentence not only loses their freedom, but is also prohibited from exercising other rights, such as being treated in a nominal and, consequently, more humane way, since they will be identified by a number related to their registration in the prison where they are being held.

This loss of identity is compounded by the practice of torture and physical aggression, according to the report of the Subcommittee on the Prevention of Torture and Other Cruel, Inhuman and Degrading Treatment or Punishment (UN, 2016), made up of experts from the United Nations Organization. The document delivered to the Brazilian government proves the existence of practices of rights violations and torture in Brazilian prisons, and was the result of visits to 22 penitentiaries across most of Brazil in 2016.

According to this report (UN, 2016), the inhumane treatment that inmates receive from prison guards, together with the various punishments imposed, contribute to the loss of their dignity and the degradation of their personality, in a process that does not offer any conditions to prepare them for a useful return to society.

It must be considered that the inhumane treatment already begins the moment the individual is caught committing an illegal act, before being arrested, because many police approaches do not comply with the legal requirements that guide the process of detaining people caught committing a crime, a fact reported by the representative of the UN High Commissioner for Human Rights in South America, Dr. Americo

Incalcaterra, in an interview with Exame magazine (SANTOS, 2017). Thus, before being brought to trial and, therefore, before being subjected to the subhuman conditions of prison, these people already receive undignified treatment that goes against the basic principles of human rights.

Both the UN Report on the Prevention of Torture (UN, 2016) and the UN High Commissioner's Office point to the lack of preparation and qualification of prison officers, also known as jailers, to deal with risky situations involving prisoners, which favors the abuse of physical force and the use of violence in everyday prison life, especially after riots or rebellions.

In these post-rebellion situations, the rigorous treatment of prisoners is considered normal and necessary, and in many cases ends up resulting in deaths, due to summary executions, as for example occurred in 1992, in the Sao Paulo House of Detention, known as Carandiru, where, after a riot, 111 prisoners were executed, a fact that has already been portrayed in books, such as *Estagdo Carandiru* (VARELLA, 2005), and in the movie *Carandiru* (BABENCO, 2003).

The report of the Subcommittee on the Prevention of Torture and Other Cruel, Inhuman and Degrading Treatment or Punishment (UN, 2016) concluded that the imposition of parallel discipline, based on violence, is a tradition in the prison environment, with illegal practices of abusive punishment not based on any legal code or prison rules. The document also shows that the use of violence is so natural that even when torture or violations of prisoners' rights are found to have taken place, the agents are not held responsible for these offenses and remain unpunished. In this way, the use of violence becomes increasingly naturalized and incorporated into the day-to-day life of the penitentiary.

In addition to the use of violence by the staff, inmates are also affected by violence practiced by the inmates themselves, such as physical attacks, sexual abuse, murder and extortion.

The cases of violence between prisoners stem from the fact that there is no physical or geographical separation between dangerous prisoners, those sentenced to long terms, and primitive prisoners, those who have served a relatively short time.

This forced coexistence, with no criteria for separating prisoners according to their dangerousness, favors the permanence of criminal gangs inside prisons, which create a parallel hierarchy that demands obedience to their rules.

Despite the proven existence of criminal organizations that hold power inside prisons (MOREIRA, 2012; BIONDI, 2014), their members are not denounced and when they are, they remain unpunished for the illegal acts committed, because in addition to the *'law of the strongest'*, the *'law of silence'* also prevails in prisons.

At the same time as what happens in prisons, there is the problem of prisoners serving time in police stations, which are unsuitable establishments for serving time under a closed regime, because they deprive prisoners of their rights, since they don't offer the conditions for prisoners to study or work, and consequently have their sentence reduced as a result of remission, as well as making it impossible for them to earn any income, which would allow them to buy products for personal use, which are not offered, but are normally allowed, by the police district management.

Despite the fact that police districts are unsuitable for serving sentences of deprivation of liberty, this is due to the inadequacy of prisons to cope with an ever-increasing demand for prisoners. Police stations also face the problem of prisoner overcrowding because, in addition to having a reduced number of cells, police districts are not legally designed to carry out custodial sentences.

One factor that has greatly contributed to the worsening of the Brazilian prison scenario is the implementation of the Hedonious Crimes Law (BRASIL, 1990a), because the various crimes listed therein, such as murder, drug trafficking and kidnapping, no longer have the legal benefit of regime progression, The despair and lack of prospects for these people has led to an even greater sense of revolt, and is yet another cause for the outbreak of insurrections in penitentiaries.

All these negative factors, combined with the lack of security in prisons and the failure of the established resocialization model, result in the outbreak of two other very current problems in the Brazilian prison system: violent riots and mass escapes.

I. 1 Discussion

Law 11.343 of August 23, 2006, also known as the Anti-Drug Law (BRASIL, 2006), contributed to the worsening of the national prison scenario. The law decriminalized drug users and introduced harsher sentences for drug traffickers, increasing the minimum prison term from three to five years. Although its general purpose was to remove users from prisons, the law did not establish the amount that differentiated the two groups, leaving this decision to the free interpretation of judges, prosecutors and police officers.

According to the 2015 Parliamentary Commission of Inquiry into the Brazilian Prison System (DOS DEPUTADOS, 2015), in the first 9 years of implementation of this law (BRASIL, 2006), the proportion of the population imprisoned for trafficking rose from 14% to 27%, making it the biggest cause of imprisonment in Brazil. Among men, 25% are imprisoned as a result of this crime, while among women, the percentage rises to 63%. The number of female prisoners has almost doubled since the new law was passed. To give you an idea, in 2005, 34% of the female prison population was responsible for crimes related to trafficking (DOS DEPUTADOS, 2015).

In an article written for *"Sur - Revista Internacional de Direitos Humanos",* Luciana Boiteux (2015), who holds a doctorate in criminal law, states that *"despite the widespread acceptance (and ratification) of drug control conventions by countries, the desired objectives of reducing consumption, preventing production and eradicating substances have not been achieved, even though incarceration rates for drug crimes are high in most countries, especially in Latin America."*

II. Rebellions and mass prison escapes in 2017

Organized uprisings carried out in a violent manner, such as those that occurred in the first fifteen days of 2017, which resulted in a total of 131 dead prisoners, aim to draw public attention to the demands made by the prison population, which range from improving food and reducing overcrowding to demanding the separation of rival criminal groups.

Although based on observations and studies carried out ten years ago, the work entitled "*The current reality of the Brazilian penitentiary system*" (ASSIS, 2007), presents a very up-to-date view of the problematic issue of escapes and rebellions in penitentiaries, which indicates that the delicate situation of Brazilian prisons remains unsolved. According to this work

> [...] the prison riots and escapes that we see on a daily basis are a response and at the same time a warning to the authorities about the inhumane conditions to which they are subjected, despite the existing protective legislation. In addition to the violation of rights within the prison, it draws attention to the ineffectiveness of the system for re-socializing prison inmates since, on average, 90% of ex-offenders return to crime and end up going back to prison (ASSIS, 2007, p. 74).

Earlier this year, the state of Amazonas suffered three prisoner massacres: at the Anisio Jobim Penitentiary Complex[3] , at the Puraquequara Prison Unit and at the Raimundo Vidal Pessoa Prison - in which 67 prisoners were murdered; Roraima's largest prison, the Monte Cristo Agricultural Penitentiary, left a toll of 33 prisoners dead; in Rio Grande do Norte, at the Alcaguz Penitentiary, a riot resulted in 26 prisoners being murdered; the Romero Nobrega Penitentiary, in the state of Paraiba, resulted in 2 deaths; in Alagoas, a riot at the Maceio House of Custody resulted in 2 deaths; in Curitiba, riots at the Piraquara Penitentiary complex resulted in 2 deaths; in Sao Paulo, a riot at the Tupi Paulista Closed Regime Penitentiary resulted in another 2 deaths.

Taking advantage of the lack of security in prisons and cases of corruption

[3] The confrontation between the Familia do Norte (FDN) and Primeiro Comando da Capital (PCC) factions at the Anisio Jobim Penitentiary Complex in Manaus took place between Sunday afternoon, 01/01/17, and the morning of 02/01/2017. It is considered by experts and professionals in the field of prison security to be the second largest massacre to have taken place in a prison at once since the Carandiru Massacre in Sao Paulo in 1992.

practiced by police officers and prison security agents, prison escapes are a constant in the current context of the Brazilian prison system.

A riot at the Professor Noe Azevedo Penitentiary Progression Center in Bauru ended in the escape of 152 prisoners on January 24, 2017; in Santa Catarina, between February 6 and 12, sixteen prisoners escaped, eight from the Blumenau Penitentiary and eight from the Vale do Itajai Penitentiary Complex; in Florianopolis, two inmates escaped from the State Penitentiary; in Rio Grande do Sul, six inmates escaped from the Sarandi State Prison on February 17; and on March 13, 32 inmates escaped after a riot at the Aparecida de Goiania Prison Complex in Goias.

The most recent mass inmate escape took place on January 24, 2017, at the Bauru Agricultural Penal Institution, a unit that houses around 1,500 inmates, from which 152 inmates escaped after a riot.

II. 1 Brief history of the main rebellions that preceded the events of 2017

The year 2006 was the most violent in terms of the number of rebellions and attacks on security forces, due to the synchronicity of the actions planned by the organized crime that reigns inside Brazilian prisons. These planned actions have caught the attention of many public security experts who are concerned about the organizational capacity of organized crime. In order to present chronologically the events orchestrated in May 2006, we will list the dates and the units that rebelled during this period:

May 11, 2006: Marcos William Herbas Camacho, the *'Marcola'*, the PCC's top leader, was transferred from Avare prison to Presidente Venceslau. Another 700 criminals linked to the faction were also transferred. The government announced that it had uncovered a plan by the group to carry out a wave of rebellions the following weekend, during Mother's Day.

13 of May: 30 people were killed and 25 injured in a series of 64 attacks, committed between the night of the 12th and the afternoon of the 13th, against police officers, civil guards and prison guards. Police barracks, police stations and bases also became targets for gunfire. The attacks were concentrated in Greater Sao Paulo, but there were

also reports inland and on the coast. At the same time, the state began to face a mega-rebellion in prisons. An estimated 24,472 inmates from 24 units joined the movement, taking 129 hostages. The police arrested 17 suspects and called in the entire police force to step up patrols.

14 May: The attacks gained momentum. Eight buses were set on fire and the number of attacks attributed to the PCC rose to 103, with 72 deaths and 27 injured. Prison riots broke out in 69 of the 105 prisons, with 300 hostages. The state government went on the counter-attack and announced the death of 19 alleged criminals between the 13th and 14th.

15 May: Sao Paulo experienced a Monday of panic as transport services were disrupted, affecting the daily lives of five million people. In 24 hours, 51 buses were attacked and set on fire. Businesses and banks closed their doors early, schools and colleges suspended classes, while the number of attacks reached 150 cases, with 96 deaths and 55 injured. The fear was accompanied by a wave of rumors, which led the police to empty Congonhas airport on suspicion of a bomb. In the evening, after 73 hours, the government announced the end of the riots in all prison units. The state administration has not confirmed an official agreement with Willians Herbas Camacho, *'Marcola', the* top leader of the *PCC - Primeiro Comando da Capital (First Command of the Capital), who* is currently in the Maximum Security Penitentiary of Presidente Bernardes.

16 May: The city of Sao Paulo had a day of relative calm, with two bus attacks recorded. The Secretariat of Penitentiary Administration complied with prisoners' requests and bought 60 television sets for the communal areas of the prisons - one of the demands made by prisoners for peace to continue in the state. The *'PCC'* released a manifesto criticizing the transfer of inmates during the early hours of *the* morning, which was classified as a *"selfish attitude by the government and authorities who are only looking out for their own political success"*.

17 May: The purchase of a copy of the testimony of the director of Deic, the São Paulo Civil Police, Godofredo Bittencourt Filho, by the PCC for R$200 was discovered. The delegate gave information in a closed session in the Chamber of

Deputies in which he said he knew of plans for attacks by the faction in May. This illegally obtained information would have enabled the criminal group to anticipate and better plan the attacks.

May 19: Cell phone network antennas were disconnected in regions of six state prisons. The government tightened its grip on the PCC. Organizations called for an investigation into excesses on the part of the Military Police in operations that left people dead in reaction to the faction's attacks.

In 2010, 18 prisoners were killed by a rival group in a rebellion at the Pedrinhas prison complex. Of these, 15 were murdered in the Sao Luis prison, which is considered maximum security. Another three deaths occurred in the Pedrinhas Penitentiary, located next to the prison, which had an attempted rebellion.

Between November and December 2013, an action aimed at exterminating members of a rival faction was carried out by inmates at the Pedrinhas Penitentiary Complex in Maranhao, 22km from the capital, Sao Luis. Twenty-two people were killed. The episode shocked the country because the perpetrators of the massacre filmed the killing, showing bodies without heads while gloating. The case led to an investigation into abuses in the prison and even cases of cannibalism were reported. It was also discovered that, over the course of that year, around 60 prisoners had been killed in the unit, which, built to house 1,700 people, had 2,500 inmates at the time.

II. 2 Discussion

Many texts have already been written about Brazil's delicate prison problem, addressing relevant aspects of the issue. A criminal justice system that claims to be a court of law, but in practice acts as if it were an administrative body, as is often the case with the Electoral Justice itself - and the way in which the rendering of accounts is interpreted is a good example - certainly bears a considerable share of responsibility, This includes the tolerance of a certain private legal profession, which not infrequently tolerates violations or fails to take all measures to reverse illegalities, which often start with a flagrante made without a police officer, and go through police corruption to allow favors to be obtained; or even public ones, such as the Public Defender's Office[4] and the State Attorney's Offices[5] and the Union Attorney's Office[6] - the former because they often fail to fulfill their role of visiting prisoners and promoting more effective measures to protect their rights; the latter because they often tolerate and try to justify in an argumentative way incomprehensible and despicable state positions to deal with the problem.

There is also a certain amount of responsibility on the part of members of the Public Prosecutor's Office and the Judiciary, who insist on pre-trial detention in order to safeguard public order or on the sole basis of the type of crime committed, who do not give due consideration to incidents of over-execution and deviation in execution, who deny the right to progression when the State itself is to blame for offering the right regime and, fundamentally, who, even though they undoubtedly have supervisory powers, allow pre-trial or final prisoners to be housed in overcrowded prisons (public or outsourced) without the slightest condition to collect human beings, under the supposed protection of the state, in the name of an unreasonable consequentialist vision, which ends up encouraging the omission of funding and maintenance of adequate public policies for criminal execution.

Lacan (1975) already said that jouissance should not be identified with pleasure for pleasure's sake, but as pleasure provided by the displeasure of the other, a situation that is unfortunately present in the collective imagination of many Brazilians who, unaware of even a minimal understanding of the meaning of human rights, not only bet on the *'return of the military',* but also argue that imprisoned Brazilians, whether

---

[4]Since everyone, without exception, has the right to access to justice, the state guarantees citizens with limited financial resources a public lawyer; the so-called public defender. The Public Defender's Office is a public institution that provides free legal assistance to people who cannot afford it. People in need, disadvantaged minority groups, as well as children and adolescents, can turn to the Public Defender's Office. The idea is to exercise human and fundamental rights. The Ombudsman's Office is also involved in out-of-court settlements (when they haven't yet become lawsuits).

[5] The State Attorney General's Office (PGE) is the institution responsible for state advocacy, i.e. representing the state in court and providing legal advice and counsel to the executive branch.

[6] The Office of the Attorney General of the Union is a senior management body of the Office of the Attorney General of the Union, an institution that represents the Union in and out of court, and reports directly and immediately to the Attorney General of the Union.

they have been tried or not, do not have the right to enjoy healthy and dignified conditions during the time they are deprived of their liberty, a discursive violence that, of course, pays its price to increase the already accentuated social inequality that we have on the streets.

The criminal factions that operate in prisons as large gangs or cartels, in fact, do nothing more than take advantage of the state's abandonment and cynicism to propagate a discourse that, because of the context mentioned above, increases the possibility of new members joining.

In addition to what can be done at local level, including the peremptory removal of prisoners from police stations, the prohibition of overcrowding in the prison system, the removal of the *'pŭbлica order'* as a non-instrumental and procedural basis for pre-trial detention, the rejection of outsourcing in the prison system, the revision of a criminal policy that.., despite some progress made in the justice system - such as the decriminalizing measures of plea bargaining and conditional suspension of proceedings - there is still an exaggerated criminalization in exalting criminal law and criminal procedure as solutions to all problems, betting on the maximum Criminal State and Criminal Procedure alongside a minimum Social State when, as Luigi Ferrajoli (1996) rightly warns, the logic should be reversed.

As long as this important thing called 'penal execution' is an *'ugly duckling'* for Brazilian law and society, and a place for bureaucrats and civil servants to hide from the responsibilities that only an engaged and committed approach to the rights of the prisoner as an excluded and marginalized *'other'* can change, there will be no way out.

There are many alternatives for overcoming this historic impasse, which has already been recognized by the Supreme Court[7] as an *'unconstitutional state of*

The Federal Supreme Court is the apex body of the Judiciary and is primarily responsible for guarding the Constitution, as defined in Article 102 of the Constitution of the Republic. It is made up of eleven Justices, all born Brazilians (art. 12, § 3, inc. IV, CF/1988), chosen from among citizens over 35 and under 65 years of age, of outstanding legal knowledge and unblemished reputation (art. 101 CF/1988), and appointed by the President of the Republic, after approval of the choice by an absolute majority of the Federal Senate (art. 101, sole paragraph, CF/1988). One of its main duties is to rule on direct actions for the unconstitutionality of federal or state laws or regulations, declaratory actions for the constitutionality of federal laws or regulations, arguments for non-compliance with fundamental precepts arising from the Constitution itself and extradition *affairs'*, albeit in a much more symbolic and punctual way than an effective one, since the Supreme Court has had several opportunities to ensure that, as the institution that represents the Judiciary at its highest level, the situation could be different.

Investing in a different way of selecting and training the state authorities working on the issue, so that they have a closer, more direct and more sensitive perception of the problems, investing and betting on the participatory-deliberative nature of democracy[8] present in the Community Councils and other collegiate bodies related to the issue, encouraging and stimulating transformative projects for life in prison, as Carmela Grune and her supporters have been doing so brilliantly for a long time with the *"Direito no Carcere"* program[9] in Porto Alegre's Central Prison, are just a few of the many other possible alternatives capable of generating good results.

In chaos and barbarism, you always have to look for *"alternatives of alternatives"*, as Boaventura de Sousa Santos (1999) teaches. After all, *"we are not at the end of history"* and the capitalist system will continue to produce (and in the case of outsourcing, profit) and manage prisoners.

Guaranteeing a prisoner's right means guaranteeing society's right to receive this prisoner back, if not in better conditions, at least not in worse conditions than those obtained since the tormenting entry into prison. Depriving life is worse than depriving liberty: When both situations occur in succession and under the tutelage of the state, then the end may well be in sight, but, like any crisis, the moment we are experiencing

---

requested by a foreign state.

[8] One of the ways of exercising participatory democracy *is* the so-called deliberative democracy, which emphasizes the different processes of public participation in decision-making during the deliberation phase. In this scenario of participatory deliberation, organized civil society plays a central role as interlocutors with public authorities. Deliberative democracy argues that the exercise of citizenship extends beyond mere participation in the electoral process, demanding more direct participation by individuals in the realm of the public sphere, in a continuous process of discussion and reflexive criticism of social norms and values.

[9] It began on August 17, 2011, in Gallery E1 of the Porto Alegre Central Prison, providing access to justice, culture, memory and information. Since its implementation, the humanistic practice has reached more than two thousand people, including more than 454 inmates and their families. It encourages the recovery of self-esteem and dignity, with repercussions on the family and society, through cultural activities integrating knowledge of Law, Art, Neuroscience and Technology. It encourages the expression of citizenship in prison, given the repressive culture, stimulated by the popularization of criminal law, which prefers to isolate rather than include. It created Brazil's first virtual platform for inmates to express themselves.

allows us to rethink and revise our paths, which could make all the difference, especially if the media, with the undeniable power it has, do not forget and *'castrate'* the problematic and relevant potential of the subject, in search of the next sensationalist headline or when the *'recess'* of the Legislative and Judicial branches in their daily activities is over or the main sports championships resume their activities.

The media, in the daily discursive and intersubjective construction that forms 'opinion' (unfortunately much more towards hatred of the prisoner than disgust with the state's omission in the face of the problem - and the way in which the cost of the prisoner is exploited or the supposedly exaggerated social security benefits for his family are distorted shows this) can indeed play a decisive role in changing the attitude of the justice system and society itself towards the issue. This is the least that could be expected from the media in a time of democracy, but unfortunately, today this is much closer to fantasy and delusion than to a probable and feasible reality.

III. Health care in prisons

The overcrowding of cells, together with the structural precariousness and insalubrity of the place, make prisons a prone environment for the spread of diseases and epidemics.

Silva (2016), in his research entitled *"Immunological study and pathological manifestations in individuals deprived of their liberty"*, found that conditions such as the unhealthiness of the environment, the precariousness of the facilities and the overcrowding of the cells, turn prisons into environments that are totally favorable to the contagion and proliferation of various diseases.

In addition to the above factors, and thus further aggravating the poor state of prison units, there is the poor food offered to inmates, the lack of hygiene, drug use and the constant riots, which mean that prisoners who entered the prison system in a relatively healthy condition leave with, at the very least, compromised psychic or organ health, due to their stay in an environment with such inhumane conditions.

Many inmates have very poor physical and emotional health, developing serious cases of depression (PINESE, 2008) and other mental disorders (MARQUES, 2013), or are affected by diseases that are difficult to treat, such as tuberculosis (SANCHEZ, 2007; BORGES, 2014; LIMA, 2015) and AIDS (SANTOS, 2002; BEZERRA, 2015).

As a result of weakened organ resistance due to the unsanitary conditions in prison, many inmates also suffer from severe cases of pneumonia (BONATTO, 2015) and hepatitis (GUIMARAES, 1998).

According to the studies *"HIV AIDS and other sexually transmitted infections in the Brazilian prison population: a systematic review" (BEZERRA, 2015) and "AIDS in prison - double victimization" (SANTOS, 2002),* approximately twenty percent of Brazilian prisoners have the HIV virus, due to promiscuity in prison environments, which translates into massive drug use and sexual abuse, aggravated by overcrowded cells.

Not to mention the lack of accessibility mechanisms for sentenced people with physical disabilities, contrary to Law No. 13.146 (BRASIL, 2015a), which provides for accessibility conditions for people with disabilities.

The incompatibility between a physical structure that favors accessibility and the structural needs of security and limited circulation in prison units is a determining factor in understanding and possibly solving this issue of prisoner health.

The determinants of the health of prisoners are affected by the neglect of the physical aspects of Brazilian prisons. Therefore, the prison as a dwelling translates into the space where health is most vulnerable. In this sense, Simone Cynamon Cohen *et al.* state that:

> The implementation of healthy spaces depends on the development of healthy public policies. Policies drawn up from the study and reflection on the reading of physical space, whether macro urban or micro housing, which promotes greater identity with the local reality and greater visibility for individual and collective aspirations and desires, adding and incorporating the concept of healthy housing (COHEN *et al.,* 2007, p. 197).

With regard to the other negative aspects of health care in prisons, we have inmates' dental treatment, which is limited to tooth extractions. There are very few cases in which the inmate can afford dental treatment in private clinics and, when they can, they are unable to transfer to such clinics, because the transportation and movement of inmates is primarily for emergency health cases.

This is due to the fact that, for any transport of prisoners, there is a legal requirement for a police escort, which prioritizes cases of court hearings or emergency medical care, where there is a risk of death of the prisoner, because the military police depend on the availability of police officers, which results in yet another obstacle that makes it impossible for the inmate to be attended to in his health needs.

Medical treatment, carried out inside prisons, consists of prescribing medication for anxiety and quick care, such as bandages and blood pressure control medication (CAPITANI, 2012).

As a result of this bleak picture, there is another serious point, perhaps the most emblematic, regarding the right to health of sentenced prisoners, because even when they manage to be taken to a hospital, they run the risk of there being no room for them, or when there is, the hospital has to have a cell with bars and padlocks for patients coming from the prison system.

All these obstacles to the right to health of prisoners result in a double penalty:

the sentence that the inmate serves in such adverse conditions, and the worsening of his health condition, which deteriorates the longer he lives in the unhealthy conditions of Brazilian prisons without the necessary medical treatment.

This set of factors that make it difficult and impossible for individuals deprived of their liberty to have access to health care is a failure to comply with the provisions of the Penal Execution Law (BRASIL, 1984), supplemented by Law 12.376 (BRASIL, 2010), which, in article 40, item VII, provides for the legal obligation of the state to attend to the prisoner's right to health care. Despite this legal provision, article 117, item II, specifically states that the sentence of prisoners with serious illnesses should be converted into a home sentence.

However, this legal determination is also not met, because among the prison population, there is a large number of inmates suffering from the most serious illnesses, as was found in the work *"Immunological studies and pathological manifestations in individuals deprived of their liberty"* (SILVA, 2016), and in the research *"Tragic absence: the late emergence of health issues in the prison environment"* (BONATTO, 2015).

In this sense, the sentence loses its resocialization character, because the sentenced person's permanence with serious illnesses that are difficult to treat, directly influences their social rehabilitation process, due to the nonconformity and revolt that are generated by not meeting their basic health treatment needs.

The legality of the right to health is also laid down in the Law of Introduction to the Civil Code, Article 5, which is also applied to the criminal sphere, and consequently to criminal enforcement, and which prescribes that *"in applying the law, the judge shall take into account the social purposes to which it is directed and the requirements of the common good"* (BRASIL, 2010).

IV. Recidivism and the ineffectiveness of the current resocialization model

The conditions under which prisoners are sentenced to deprivation of liberty do not provide effective support for the true re-socialization of convicts, since, according to the latest survey by the Institute for Applied Economic Research (BRASIL, 2015b), the recidivism rate among prisoners is 24.4%, i.e. one in four ex-convicts returns to prison in less than five years.

This regrettable reality of the national prison landscape is a direct consequence of the conditions and treatment that prisoners have been subjected to while serving their sentences, with the aggravating factor that, even when they are released, society receives them with indifference and rejection, which makes the prospect of freedom rather bleak.

Due to the helplessness of the authorities and of society itself, the ex-convict, technically called an inmate, will carry the stigma of being an ex-prisoner, which will make him more marginalized and often end up leading him back to illegal practices because he can't find better opportunities for work and a dignified life.

Paradoxically, articles 25, 26 and 27 of the Penal Execution Law (BRASIL, 1984) stipulate extensive support for convicts, through social assistance, guidance on obtaining employment and the provision of food and accommodation for the first sixty days of their release.

The body created to provide this support to the inmate is the Patronato Penitenciario[10] , whose main task is to promote the re-employment of the inmate in the job market, and to provide legal, psychological and pedagogical assistance. Despite its fundamental role in the process of social reintegration, the Patronato Penitenciario has faced a lack of political interest from state governments which, because they don't give

[10] The Patronato *is* an indispensable institution for the proper exercise of penal execution, whose primary function is to provide full and free legal assistance to prisoners and former prisoners, as well as contributing to the supervision of penal execution. It provides direct assistance to prisoners in prisons. Its activity is not limited to the mere provision of legal services, but also to the possibility of having a regular monitoring body. As for the people it assists, it is clear that they are economically disadvantaged and can easily be labeled as "forgotten people", even by the state itself.

this body its due importance, don't allocate the necessary resources to it, thus making it impossible for it to carry out its legal duties.

This means that society and the authorities must recognize the importance of a policy to support convicts, because everyone's awareness of the need for convicts to reintegrate into society will lead to better conditions for social reintegration and help minimize the problem of criminal recidivism.

If the national prison landscape remains as it is today, with disregard for the rules governing prison procedures, the situation will tend to get even worse, as today's unassisted inmate will continue to be tomorrow's repeat offender.

V. Adolescence in conflict

In addition to Brazil's fourth place in the world ranking of incarcerated individuals, the latest National Penitentiary Information Survey (INFOPEN, 2014) shows that 55% of Brazil's 622,202 prisoners are between 18 and 29 years old, which means that more than half of the country's prison population is in their teens and post-teens.

According to the World Health Organization (WHO, 1986) and the Pan American Health Organization (PAHO, 2012), adolescence is a biological process and organic experience in which cognitive development and personality structure accelerate, and covers pre-adolescence (between 10 and 14 years of age) and adolescence (between 15 and 19 years of age). This definition by age group, according to this literature, i.e. between 10 and 19 years of age, is simply for statistical reasons, since adolescence is considered to be a process that begins before the age of 10 and does not end at 19.

The chronological limits of adolescence according to the United Nations Organization (UN, 1955) encompass the age range of 15 to 24, although in most countries the concept of legal adulthood is established at 18, but other criteria exist and remain flexible and confusing, according to local customs and cultures.

In Brazil, the Statute of the Child and Adolescent (BRASIL, 1990b), in its article 2, defines adolescence as the phase between 12 and 18 years of age, and in exceptional cases, according to articles 121 and 142, the statute applies up to 21 years of age.

Data from the most recent Penitentiary Information Report, INFOPEN (BRAZIL, 2014), also shows that a large number of the individuals imprisoned in Brazil began their illicit activities as teenagers, and many of them have already served socio-educational measures as teenagers, as a result of having committed offenses.

This relationship between incarcerated adult individuals and their history of offending[11] in adolescence, with the consequent compliance with socio-educational

[11] The term "infracional act" was coined by the legislators when they drafted the *Statute of Children and Adolescents* (BRASIL, 1990). Thus, it is not said that the adolescent has committed a crime or

measures[12] makes clear the importance of this stage of development in the construction of values, ideas and behaviors that will influence the individual's formation process, because according to Erickson (1994) and Salles (2005) adolescence is a stage of human development in which the individual is vulnerable to the influences of the environment, as they undergo significant physical, psychological and emotional changes, and at this stage many values are challenged, rethought and modified according to the environment in which they live.

The most recent Annual Survey of SINASE - the National System for Socio-Educational Assistance (BRASIL, 2015c), points out that of the total of 201,032,714 Brazilian inhabitants in 2014, the total adolescent population corresponded to 26,154,356 people, of which 23,066 adolescents were serving custodial sentences.

More up-to-date 2016 data from the National Register of Adolescents in Conflict (CNJ, 2016) showed that twice as many adolescents were serving socio-educational measures in Brazil compared to 2014. Of the 189,000 adolescents serving socio-educational measures, 58,079 adolescents are serving deprivation and restriction of liberty measures.

Nowadays, modern society is full of violence and risk to which everyone is exposed, especially teenagers, because they have so much freedom to act, but are not properly prepared to enjoy this freedom. They depend to a large extent on their family environment.

As well as the family, the school must help with this education, but this is still done very timidly in our country, and it can be deduced that teenagers and teachers are two overlapping realities, in other words, they don't really know each other yet. Not all

---

criminal offense, but rather an infraction. Article 103 of this law states that "conduct described as a crime or criminal offense is considered to be an infraction". Therefore, an infraction is a reprehensible act of disrespect for the rules, public order, property or the rights of citizens, committed by minors.

[12] Socio-educational measures are applicable to adolescents who have committed offenses and are provided for in article 112 of the Statute of Children and Adolescents (BRASIL, 1990). Although they are a response to the commission of a crime, they have a predominantly educational and non-punitive nature. They are aimed at people between the ages of 12 and 18, and may exceptionally be applied to young people up to the age of 21, as provided for in Article 2 of the aforementioned document.

parents, nor all educators, are prepared for the mission of educating, which is more complex than simply informing.

The rights gained by adolescents are undoubtedly positive. However, all of this must be done responsibly, so that the misuse of freedom doesn't lead them into situations that are definitely damaging, even at the beginning of their lives, and which can be perpetuated into adulthood, as the INFOPEN report (2014) has rightly pointed out.

The above considerations coincide with those of Oliveira (2007, p. 135-158), who considers that, for adolescents, the family is their reference point in which their life history is involved, and it is the place where they build their identity. The way in which families deal with affection, sex, interrelationships, hierarchies, religion and gender issues, as well as their place in the social hierarchy, is very important for adolescents. The family environment should be one of protection, characterized by respect, affection and a relationship of equality. When there are unstructured, authoritarian, hierarchical homes with rigid moral and sexual standards, these adolescents become more susceptible to experiencing suffering and problems.

V. 1. A brief history of the main riots and rebellions involving adolescent offenders.

The great Brazilian prison crisis has also affected the institutions responsible for enforcing socio-educational measures for adolescent offenders. In this sense, this topic will present the main occurrences of riots and revolts committed by the inmates of these institutions.

In October 1999, four teenagers were killed, one of them decapitated and two charred, during a riot at the now-defunct Imigrantes unit, in the south of the capital. This riot was the most violent recorded in the history of the now-defunct FEBEM[13] -

[13] FEBEM - State Foundation for the Welfare of Minors in the State of Sao Paulo was created in 1976 by the same manager who set up FUNABEM in 1964 in Rio de Janeiro, Mario Altenfelder. It is currently called Fundagao CASA - Centro de Atendimento Socioeducativo ao Adolescente (CASA Foundation - Center for Socio-Educational Assistance to Adolescents), and is a foundational autarchy created by the Government of the State of Sao Paulo and linked to the State Secretariat for Justice and the Defense of Citizenship. Its function is to carry out the socio-educational measures applied by the Judiciary to adolescents who have committed offenses. Like FEBEM, it is aimed at adolescent offenders between the ages of 12 and 18, as determined by the Statute of the

Fundagao do Bem-Estar do Menor. More than 1,000 of Imigrantes' 1,216 offenders took 16 staff and other inmates hostage and set fire to three of the unit's buildings.

The then Secretary of Social Assistance and Development, Marta Godinho, was fired and replaced in December by Edsom Ortega, who took control of the Foundation promising to start the decentralization process.

In January 1999, FEBEM began building the Franco da Rocha facility. The site has capacity for 960 inmates and its construction caused outrage among representatives of civil society, members of human rights organizations and also the prosecutors of the Child and Youth Court. Ortega said that the units would be small, but within a large complex.

In April of the same year, the secretariat admitted that it was renovating the Parelheiros prison, in the south zone, to house inmates from the jails and the COC. The news also provoked a reaction from prosecutors, who obtained a court injunction prohibiting the transfer. The injunction has now been lifted.

At the beginning of November, the inmates of Imigrantes were transferred to Pinheiros Prison, in the west of Sao Paulo, and Santo Andre Prison, in the ABC region, and to the COC (Centro de Observagao Criminologica), in Carandiru, in the north. The government then promised that the transfer to prison systems, which is forbidden by the ECA (BRASIL, 1990), would be an emergency measure and the young people would soon be transferred.

Two months after they were put in the jails, the young people who were there had still not been transferred. The Secretary of State promised to transfer them to Parelheiros prison, in the far south of the city, as early as that week. Both the prospect of transfer to Parelheiros and Franco da Rocha caused the teenagers to revolt, and they staged several rebellions and riots in an attempt to prevent the transfers.

On December 26, 1999, a teenager was beaten to death by other inmates at Santo Andre Prison in São Paulo.

January 5, 2000 was marked by the escape of inmates from Santo Andre Prison, in the ABC region of the state of Sao Paulo. This escape became famous for being the

---

Child and Adolescent (BRASIL, 1990b).

third time that minors had escaped from this unit, and for the daring and courage of the inmates in jumping over a wall more than 3 meters high without the aid of any tool or mechanism that would enable such an escape.

On January 14, 2000, ten inmates of Santo Andre Prison rebelled and took six monitors hostage.

On January 18, a three-hour riot left two injured and caused a lot of damage to the FEBEM building in Ribeirao Preto (319 km from São Paulo). The minors took two monitors hostage. An intern suffered a cut to the head and a monitor was injured in the face.

On January 24, 2000, a group of 23 inmates managed to escape from Santo Andre Prison. They escape through the front door.

On January 31st of the same year, five armed men broke into the FEBEM unit in Jardim Robru, in the east of Sao Paulo, and rescued 11 minors.

On February 5, 2000, eleven FEBEM employees were held hostage during a rebellion at the Franco da Rocha facility (40 km from Sao Paulo). The inmates were armed with wooden and iron stones.

On February 20, 2000, a riot at the FEBEM unit in Tatuape, in the southeast of Sao Paulo, left at least 27 people injured, including 22 inmates. The riot destroyed a large part of the Tatuape Foundation's facilities.

On February 21, 2000, seventeen teenagers, all aged 18, who took part in the rebellion at FEBEM Tatuape were indicted at the 81st Police Station (Belem) on charges of attempted murder, damage and gang formation.

On March 1, 2000 - Six minors escaped from Febem Raposo Tavares, on the west side of the city. A power cut in the unit facilitated the escape of six minors. In Campinas, at least ten teenagers escaped from a FEBEM unit.

On March 8, 2000, 50 young people escaped from FEBEM Tatuape. Two days later, and for the second day running, the juvenile offenders in the Tatuape unit rebelled. Two managed to escape.

On March 11, 2000, FEBEM Tatuape had another rebellion. Around 60 inmates from 3 of the 22 units in Tatuape, Sao Paulo, rebelled. They burned mattresses and climbed onto the roofs of the unit.

On March 25, 2000, three teenagers escaped from FEBEM in Guaruja, on the coast of São Paulo, three days after the unit started operating. The newly refurbished building, with 72 places, had received its first group of 14 inmates two days earlier. On March 27, 2000, 22 inmates escaped from FEBEM Tatuape.

On March 28, 2000, 59 inmates of the FEBEM in Itaim Paulista, on the east side of the city, rebelled. None of them managed to escape.

On April 15, 2000, around 300 minors from Santo Andre prison rebelled after an escape attempt. The riot took place in protest against their transfer to the Parelheiros prison.

On April 16, 2000, technical reports indicated that around 900 FEBEM inmates, considered to be highly dangerous, were subjected to mistreatment and subhuman living conditions. In the Pinheiros jail, the lack of hygiene even affects the outpatient clinic. Boys said that clothes were stored on the floor and changed only once a month. Up to 60 people shared one bar of soap. At least five teenagers escaped from the Raposo Tavares unit.

On April 19, 2000, prosecutors from Sao Paulo's Childhood and Youth Court confirmed that the Parelheiros prison, in the south zone, was unsuitable for housing adolescent offenders, after a visit to the site. The National Human Rights Movement and the Center for the Defense of Children and Adolescents also denounced the prison's conditions.

On April 24, 2000, adolescents from Santo Andre Prison started a new rebellion. Around 230 inmates, armed with sticks and iron bars, burned down part of the building, occupied the roof, set up barricades at the entrance to the prison and took 12 staff members hostage. They were protesting against their transfer to Parelheiros prison.

On May 2, 2000, inmates at FEBEM in Tatuape rioted for more than two hours. At least four adolescents escaped. A monitor was injured. The youths did not want to be transferred to Parelheiros prison. The State Secretariat for Assistance and Development managed to suspend the injunction prohibiting the transfer of inmates to the Parelheiros prison and 69 inmates from FEBEM Tatuape were transferred to Franco da Rocha, where there were already around 200 young people.

On May 7, 2000, the Franco da Rocha unit faced its first rebellion.

On May 8, 2000, in the late afternoon, the infernos started a new rebellion in the Franco da Rocha unit. Around 100 infernos started a riot at Santo Andre Prison, in the ABC region of Sao Paulo. Four minors escaped from the FEBEM unit in Guaruja. Two guards and three shift coordinators were convicted of facilitating an escape and malfeasance.

On May 15, 2000, minors from the Franco da Rocha unit carried out their third rebellion in two weeks of operation. It was the first time that inmates had escaped from the unit. Of the 40 who escaped, 23 had been recaptured by early evening.

On May 16, 2000, more than a hundred minors from the FEBEM unit in Franco da Rocha rioted at around 7pm. At least five staff members and one minor were injured in the riot. It was the fourth riot at the unit since its inauguration on May 2.

On May 27, 2000, the Guaruja unit recorded another rebellion at around 9pm. Twenty-one teenagers broke down the door of the accommodation where they were staying, reached the kitchen of the complex and started breaking furniture, household appliances and other utensils. One minor managed to escape.

On May 29, 2000, a group of high-risk teenagers from the Tatuape unit clashed with monitors at around midnight on Monday (29). No escape was recorded, no one was injured and the situation was under control by 1am.

On the morning of June 2, 2000, around 50 minors started a new rebellion in the Tatuape unit. The inmates set fire to at least three pavilions. There are no reports of any escapes.

On June 5, 2000, three teenagers escaped from the FEBEM unit in Campinas on Sunday night. Two others tried to escape but were recaptured. Since January of that year, 52 teenagers have escaped in 12 incidents.

On June 23, 2000, twenty-five adolescents from the FEBEM units in Itaim Paulista (east of Sao Paulo), Raposo Tavares and Campinas escaped on the night of the 22nd and 23rd.

On July 3, 2000, five teenagers escaped from the Campinas FEBEM (formerly Unipai) after beating up two monitors with stilettos. A riot broke out. No one was injured.

On July 23, 2000, around 130 inmates rioted at the Parelheiros facility, in the south of Sao Paulo. During the riot, the inmates held two staff members hostage.

On August 9, 2000, around 100 juvenile offenders rioted at the Franco da Rocha facility, in Greater Sao Paulo. At around 10.30pm, the minors in one of the wings of UE-31 set fire to mattresses and partially destroyed the living quarters. Armed with sticks and stones, the minors climbed onto the roofs of the unit and threatened a mass escape.

On August 10, 2000, six minors escaped from the Ribeirao Preto unit (319 km from Sao Paulo).

On November 14, 2000, the FEBEM Raposo Tavares unit, in the southwest of Sao Paulo, recorded a mass escape. According to the organization's press office, all 85 inmates tried to escape.

On December 20, 2000, the FEBEM unit in Parelheiros, on the south side of Sao Paulo, recorded an escape of 163 juvenile offenders. This was the largest number since October 1999, when around 360 adolescents escaped from the Imigrantes Complex in one go.

Inside and outside the state of Sao Paulo, and also in Brazil, the State Foundation for the Welfare of Minors has become notorious for escapes, rebellions, reports of ill-treatment of adolescents, torture and overcrowding. In 2003 alone, 80 rebellions were recorded in its units. In 2005, there were 53, 18 of them in Tatuape, the largest complex at the time, which housed 1,800 adolescents, around 20% of the young people then detained in the state.

Numerous complaints were sent to the Public Prosecutor's Office, the Organization of American States (OAS) and various other human rights organizations. FEBEM made the national and international news, revealing the abuses against the lives of these adolescents and their no less violent reactions. The crisis of those years culminated in a change in the institution's presidency and new management guidelines. The name also changed. A bill was passed in December 2006 and, since then, adolescents serving socio-educational sentences have been cared for by the CASA Foundation.

In June 2005, president Alexandre Moraes was replaced by Berenice Maria Giannella, after dismissing 1,751 employees in an attempt to end torture within FEBEM. Of these, 540 were reinstated after a decision by the Sao Paulo Court of Justice, and another 923 through a decision by the Federal Supreme Court (STF) in April 2007. During his administration, he took a series of decisions to try to reverse this scenario, such as the decentralization of the units, with the construction of new buildings, and the decommissioning of the large complexes.

The Tatuape megacomplex was shut down and, since 2006, 59 buildings have been built. Most of them are designed to house up to 56 teenagers in each unit. But complexes like those in Bras, with five buildings and capacity for 1,300 young people, Franco da Rocha and Raposo Tavares, for example, are still active, with a new name, a new presidency and new units.

And even with so many changes, a lot still happens between the walls of the Foundation, and is kept there. As if in a vicious circle of silence, reports of mistreatment, high doses of medication and violence are considered commonplace by the inmates and people who work or serve time there.

FINAL CONSIDERATIONS

The increase in the number of prisoners in Brazil, although very worrying, is not a recent phenomenon, and can be better understood and quantified by taking into account the incarceration rate considered acceptable by the International Center for Prison Studies[14] , of King's College London, which is up to 150 prisoners per 100,000 inhabitants. With the fourth largest prison population in the world, Brazil has an incarceration rate of 300 prisoners per 100,000 inhabitants.

Detentions under the Hedonated Crimes Law (BRASIL, 1990a), in which convictions for drug trafficking account for 28% of the prison population (INFOPEN, 2014), were mainly responsible for this increase in the number of people imprisoned, a movement that has been called the *"great incarcerationC"* (FOUCAULT, 1999).

The number of people imprisoned and sentenced for drug trafficking is largely due to the lack of objective criteria for differentiating between trafficking and personal use, as well as for defining the quantity of drugs. Law 11.343, known as the *"Anti-Drug Law"* (BRASIL, 2006), treats those who are criminalized as drug traffickers with extreme rigour, making it impossible to take a series of measures that could lead to decarceration and a reduction in prison overcrowding.

The current national incarceration policy represents a flagrant disregard for domestic and international rules that deal with issues related to penal execution, aggravating the problems of health care, cell overcrowding, rebellions and escapes, because only with measures to decarcerate and decriminalize can the rapid pace of national prison population growth be slowed down.

The negative effects of this policy are compounded by the delay in granting benefits to prisoners who are already entitled to progression, such as transfer to semi-open regime units or release for those who have already completed their sentence. In

[14] The International Center for Prison Studies, ICPS, was established in 1997 at King's College London and seeks to help governments and other relevant agendas develop appropriate policies on prisons and the use of imprisonment.

[15] Michel Foucault used the term "great incarceration" in his book *The History of Madness*, referring to the process of disciplining different people (the poor, criminals and the sick) that took place between the 17th and 18th centuries in Europe. Today, the term is associated with the process of expanding punitive systems, especially in the United States of America.

this way, the units of the Brazilian Penitentiary System become increasingly overcrowded, stimulating violence inside prisons, which reaches its peak in the form of riots, such as those that took place in January 2017.

Violations of a prisoner's rights, which amount to illegal restraint, are the result of inefficiency and negligence on the part of the bodies responsible for penal execution, and may even give rise to civil liability on the part of the state, due to the fact that the individual is kept in prison excessively and illegally.

An alternative to minimize prison overcrowding would be to transfer prisoners with serious health problems to hospitals within the prison system, or to serve their sentences under house arrest, because failure to comply with the provisions of article 117, item II, of the Penal Execution Law (BRASIL, 1984), which results in prisoners being kept in a deplorable state of health, within the prison environment, would be causing the sentence to lose its re-socializing character, because, in addition to encouraging the spread and proliferation of diseases, due to the large number of people sharing a small physical space, serving the sentence under house arrest would certainly contribute to alleviating the bleak picture of prison overcrowding.

With the implementation and application of legal and constitutional guarantees in the execution of sentences, the aim is not to make prisons a totally pleasant environment for human coexistence, but rather to respect and comply with the principle of legality, the basis of a Democratic State of Law, whose function is to provide conditions for the effective resocialization of individuals serving custodial sentences.

However, as long as the situation of prisoners is neglected by the state and society, turning prisons into human waste dumps, not only the prison landscape but also the problem of crime and public safety will tend to worsen.

It should not be overlooked that the overwhelming majority of the Brazilian prison population is made up of people with low purchasing power, unemployed and illiterate (INFOPEN, 2014) who, because they have not had better social opportunities, have been pushed into crime.

Even more important is the need to reflect more deeply on the consequences of this bleak prison situation, because the prisoner who currently suffers the hardships within the prison environment will tomorrow be the citizen who will be back in society, bringing with them a whole baggage of traumas and revolts.

With regard to escapes, considering the martyrdom to which prisoners are subjected in Brazilian prisons, their attempts are understandable, because there is no other way to demand that they plan ways of escaping, in an attempt to escape not only from the physical prison environment, freedom is an irrepressible desire of the human being, and it cannot be expected that the prisoner will conform to the state of confinement on his own, especially in the way in which the deprivation of his liberty is carried out in our prison system.

The normative resolutions governing the minimum health conditions for prisoners contrast with the real and inhumane conditions present in prison environments, such as poor food, clothing restrictions (since the vast majority of prisons oblige inmates to wear only the unit's uniform, which is distributed only once and in a single quantity) and poor medical care.

By analyzing the demands and/or reasons for the riots in penitentiaries across the country, it is possible to see that the health conditions in the prison environment are far from what is acceptable in terms of human rights, since the incarcerated are permanently conditioned to a degrading environment in various aspects, starting with the physical conditions of the cells they inhabit.

Therefore, in addressing the issue of humanization in prisons, this book started from the recognition of physical, emotional and psychological health as a fundamental and human right. However, beyond its normative nature, it is understood that human rights are susceptible to change, directly related to social transformations, reflecting the values and desires of a society. Therefore, it is possible to conclude that Brazilian penitentiary institutions are still conceived as a place of suffering, characterized by overcrowded, damp and unventilated cells; lack of sanitary, electrical and plumbing facilities; poor hygiene and food conditions and a prison population susceptible to infectious diseases, also mobilized to carry out rebellions, in which they protest against such adverse conditions.

With regard to assistance for ex-offenders, its implementation should not be seen as the only solution to the problem of the high rate of recidivism among ex-offenders (BRASIL, 2015), since many of the factors that cause this problem are related to the conditions of the prison environment, which requires the adoption of a series of measures during the period of incarceration.

However, systematic work on the person of the inmate would certainly minimize the degrading effects of their stay in prison and contribute to their readaptation to social life, reducing their chances of reoffending.

The problematic issue of the large number of adolescents serving socio-educational measures of deprivation of liberty requires us to take into account this period of physical, psychological and social vulnerability, which allows adolescents to suffer influences from their culture and sub-culture, family and companions, with complex changes for the development of the human being, constituting one of the groups most sensitive to serious problems today such as hunger, poverty, malnutrition, illiteracy, prostitution, violence, abandonment, family disintegration.

Added to this is the lack of family support, illiteracy, the socio-economic poverty that affects thousands of teenagers, the current high unemployment rates and the problem of drug trafficking.

In this way, the lack of an educational system that encourages sociability, the lack of family structure, high unemployment rates and the current incarceration policy make these individuals very vulnerable, which requires professionals, both in education and those concerned with solving social difficulties, This requires professionals, both in education and those concerned with solving social difficulties, to join forces to think of possible solutions to this issue of the large contingent of juvenile offenders serving socio-educational measures of deprivation of liberty, considering that a large number of adolescents subjected to socio-educational measures end up increasing the prison contingent when they reach adulthood (INFOPEN, 2014).

This makes it extremely important for adults and professionals who work with adolescents to pay careful and, above all, affectionate attention to them, considering the vulnerability of their behavior and their need for affirmation, which are characteristic of this stage of human development.

BIBLIOGRAPHICAL REFERENCES

BABENCO, H. *Carandi.ru.* Brazil: Globo Filmes, 2003.

BARROS, A. M. de. *Citizenship and the Brazilian Penitentiary System.* Justributario, Fortaleza. v. 10, p. 1-20, 2011.

BEZERRA, A. T. A. F. *HIV/AIDS and other sexually transmitted infections in the Brazilian prison population: a systematic review.* 2015. 82 f. Dissertation (Professional Master's Degree in Public Health Epidemiology) - Oswaldo Cruz Foundation, Rio de Janeiro.

BIONDI, K. *Ethnography in the movement: territory, hierarchy and law in the PCC.* 2014 334 f. Dissertation (Doctorate in Social Anthropology) - Federal University of Sao Carlos, Sao Carlos.

BOGOTA, Inter-American Commission on Human Rights. *American Declaration of the Rights and Duties of Man.* April 1948. Available at <https://www.cidh.oas.org/basicos/portugues/b.Declaracao Americana.htm>. Accessed on March 18, 2017.

BOITEUX, L. Brazil: critical reflections on a repressive drug policy. In: Sur - International Journal of Human Rights. V. 12. N. 21, edition August 2015.

BONATTO, B. M. *Tragic absence: the late emergence of health issues in the prison environment.* 2015. 111 f. Dissertation (Master's in Applied Social Sciences) - State University of Ponta Grossa, Ponta Grossa.

BORGES, M. J. G. *Epidemiological aspects of Tuberculosis in the Prison System in Sdo Jose do Rio Preto/SP.* 2014. 58 f. Dissertation (Master's in Nursing) - Sao Jose do Rio Preto Medical School, Sao Jose do Rio Preto.

BRAZIL, Presidency of the Republic. Civil House. Sub-Cabinet for Legal Affairs. *Law No. 7.210 of July 11, 1984. Penal Execution Law.* Available at <http://www.planalto.gov.br/ccivil 03/leis/L7210.htm>. Accessed on February 12, 2017.

BRAZIL, Presidency of the Republic. Civil House. Sub-Cabinet for Legal Affairs. *Constitution of the Federative Republic of Brazil, of October 5, 1988.* Available at <http: //www.planalto .gov.br/ccivil 03/constituicao/constituicaocompilado. htm>. Accessed on February 12, 2017.

BRAZIL, Presidency of the Republic. Civil House. Sub-Cabinet for Legal Affairs. *Law No. 8.072 of July 25, 1990a.* Law on Heinous Crimes. Available at <http://www.planalto.gov.br/ccivil 03/leis/L8072.htm>. Accessed on February 14, 2017.

BRAZIL, Presidency of the Republic. Office of the Chief of Staff, Sub-Cabinet for

Legal Affairs. Law No. 8.069 of July 13, 1990b. Dispoes sobre o Estatuto da Crianga e do Adolescenteeda otrasprovidencias . Disponivelem <http://www.planalto.gov.br/ccivil 03/leis/L8069.htm>. Accessed on May 12, 2017.

BRAZIL, Presidency of the Republic. Civil House. Sub-Cabinet for Legal Affairs. *Law No. 11.343, of August 23, 2006.* Establishes the National System of Public Policies on Drugs . Available at <http://www.planalto.gov.br/ccivil 03/ato2004-2006/2006/lei/l 11343.htm>. Accessed on March 14, 2017.

BRAZIL, Presidency of the Republic. Civil House. Sub-Cabinet for Legal Affairs. *Law No. 12.376, of December 30, 2010,* supplementing the wording of Decree-Law No. 4.657, of July 4, 1942. Available at <http://www.planalto.gov.br/ccivil 03/ato2015-2018/2015/lei/l13146.htm>. Accessed on April 10, 2017.

BRAZIL, Presidency of the Republic. Civil House. *Law No. 13.146, of July 6, 2015a.* Provides for the Brazilian law on the inclusion of people with disabilities. Available at <http://www.planalto.gov.br/ccivil 03/ato2015-2018/2015/lei/l13146.htm>. Accessed on April 18, 2017.

BRAZIL, Secretariat for Strategic Affairs of the Presidency of the Republic. *Institute for Applied Economic Research,* 2015b.

BRAZIL. Presidency of the Republic. Secretariat for Human Rights . *SINASE Annual Survey 2013.* Brasilia: Human Rights Secretariat of the Presidency of the Republic, 2015c.

BRAZIL. Ministry of Justice. National Justice Council. *National Register of Adolescents in Conflict.* Brasilia, 2016.

CAPITANI, R. *The Brazilian prison environment and inmate health: a study based on the reality of the Bento Gongalvez Penitentiary.* 2012. 131 f. Dissertation (Master of Laws) - University of Caxias do Sul, Caxias do Sul.

CARVALHO, J. M. *Cidadania no Brasil: O longo caminho.* Rio de Janeiro: Brazilian Civilization, 2002.

COHEN, S. C. et al. Healthy housing and health-friendly environments as a health promotion strategy. *Ciencia e Saúde Coletiva,* v. 12, n. 1, 2007.

DOS DEPUTADOS, CAMARA. 2015 Parliamentary Commission of Inquiry into the Brazilian Prison System. Documentation and Information Center of the Library of the Chamber of Deputies, 2015.

ERIKSON, E. H. *Identity: Youth and crisis.* New York: Norton &Company,1994.

FERRAJOLI, L. Diritto e Ragione Teoria del garantismo penale, 1996.

FONTE, J. C. B. D. *Prevalence of mental disorders in women serving time in a prison in Pernambuco*. 2011. 60 f. Dissertation (Master's Degree in Forensic Expertise) - University of Pernambuco, Recife.

FOUCAULT, P. M. *Vigiar e Punir: nascimento da prisdo.* Translated by Raquel Ramalhete. Petropolis: Vozes, 1999.

GOFFMAN, E. *Asylums, prisons and convents.* Translated by Dante Moreira Leite. Sao Paulo: Perspectiva, 1974.

GUIMARAES, T. *Seroepidemiology of the hepatitis C virus and risk factors for its acquisition in the Sao Paulo House of Detention.* 1998. 55 f. Dissertation (Master's Degree in Infectious and Parasitic Diseases) - Federal University of Sao Paulo, Sao Paulo.

IBGE. *Brazilian Institute of Geography and Statistics, 2014.* Available at <http://www.ibge.gov.br/home/estatistica/populacao/estimativa2014/estimativa dou.shtm>. Accessed on March 14, 2017.

INFOPEN, Ministry of Justice. Penal Execution. *National survey of penitentiary information,* 2014.

LACAN, J. *The Seminar, Book 20: Still More.* Rio de Janeiro: Jorge Zahar, 1985.

LIMA, M. C. R. A. D. D. *Strategies for tuberculosis control in the prison system: integrative literature review.* 2015. 116 f. Dissertation (Master's in Public Health Nursing) - University of Sao Paulo, Ribeirao Preto.

MARQUES, M. M. D. S. *Crime and Drugs: A Study of São Paulo's Prison Population.* 2013. 112 f. Dissertation (Master's Degree in Psychiatry and Medical Psychology) - Federal University of Sao Paulo, Sao Paulo.

MELLO. C. D. de A. *Curso* de *direito international publico.* 13. ed. Rio de Janeiro: Renovar, 2001.

MOREIRA, A. *The PCC in São Paulo: collective of prisoners or criminal organization?* 2012. 110 f. Dissertation (Master's in Political Science) - Federal University of Sao Carlos, Sao Carlos.

OLIVEIRA, W. F. *Educagdo social de rua: bases historicas, politicas, pedagogicas.* Historia, Ciencia e Saude. N.12. v. 1: Manguinhos 2007; p.135-158.

WHO, World Health Organization. *Youth health - a change for society.* Technical report of the Study Group on Adolescents and Health for All of the World Health Organization. Geneva, 1986.

UN, United Nations General Assembly. Resolution 217 of December 10, 1948. Provisions on the Universal Declaration of Human Rights. Available at

<http: //www.ohchr.org/EN/UDHR/Documents/UDHR T ranslations/por.pdf>. Accessed on June 14, 2017.

UN, Security Council. *1st United Nations Congress on the Prevention of Crime and the Treatment of Offenders, 1955.* Available at <http: //www.direito shumano s.usp. br/index.php/Human-Rights-in-the-Administration%C3%A7%C3%A3o-da-Justi%C3%A7a.-Prote%C3%A7%C3%A3o-dos-Prisoners-e-Detidos.-Prote%C3%A7%C3%A3o-contra-a-Tortura-Maus-tratos-e-Desaparecimento/regras-minimas para-o-tratamento-dos-reclusos.html>. Accessed on April 2, 2017.

UN, Report of the Subcommittee on Prevention of Torture and Other Cruel, Inhuman and Degrading Treatment or Punishment, 2016. Available at <http://www.sdh. gov.br/noticias/pdf/relatorio-subcomite-de-prevencao-da-tortura-1>. Accessed on 26/04/2017.

OPS. *Pan American Health Organization.* 1st International Seminar on Good Practices in Adolescent Health in the Americas, 2012.

ORTH, G. M. N. *A hora e a vez dos direitos humanos: percurso histórico e insergdo dos direitos humanos no sistema penitenciario brasileiro.* Ambito Juridico, Rio Grande, n. 99, Apr. 2012.

PINESE, C. S. V. *Identifying depression in women in the prison system.* 2008. 76 f. Dissertation (Master's in Nursing) - University of Sao Paulo, Ribeirao Preto.

SALLES, L. M. F. *Childhood and adolescence in contemporary society: some notes.* Estudos de Psicologia: Campinas, 2005.

SANCHEZ, A. A. M. M. R. *Tuberculosis in the Prison Population of the State of Rio de Janeiro: prevalence and guidelines for formulating control strategies.* 2007. 80 f. Thesis (Doctorate in Public Health) - Oswaldo Cruz Foundation, Rio de Janeiro.

SANTOS, B D. S. *A discourse on the sciences.* Porto (Portugal): Afrontamento, 1999.

SANTOS, J. J. D. *AIDS in prison - double victimization.* 2002. 124 f. Dissertation (Masters in Law) - Candido Mendes University, Rio de Janeiro.

SANTOS, B. F. *UN: impunity for torture in prisons is the rule in Brazil.* EXAME.com magazine. January, 2017. Available at <http://exame.abril.com.br/brasil/onu-impunidade-por-tortura-nas-prisoes-e-regra-no-brasil/>. Accessed on: April 25, 2017.

SILVA, L. F. P. *Immunological study and pathological manifestations in individuals deprived of liberty.* 2016113 f. Dissertation (Master's Degree in Immunology and basic and applied parasitology) - Federal University of Mato Grosso, Barra do Gargas.

VARELLA, D. *Estagdo Carandiru.* Editora Companhia das Letras, 2005.

VENTURA, M. Human rights and health: possibilities and challenges. In: BRAZIL,

Ministry of Health. Oswaldo Cruz Foundation. *Saude e direitos humanos,* Brasilia, n. 07, p. 87-100. 2010.

MIX
Papier aus verantwortungsvollen Quellen
Paper from responsible sources
FSC® C105338

Printed by Books on Demand GmbH, Norderstedt / Germany